MML-001

For Beck, with love – MH

DOGS WITH JOBS

MAX HAMILTON

ALBERT STREET
BOOKS

All around the world, dogs are
known for being our best friends.
Most are pet dogs and spend their days

chasing balls,

going for walks,

snoozing

and snuggling.

But some dogs have jobs and do amazing and brave things, like protecting penguins or jumping out of helicopters to save people at sea.

Let's meet these dogs who have very important jobs!

Albie stands guard at the Opera House cafe. His job is to stop seagulls from stealing people's food from their plates! He wears special shoes so his paws don't get burnt on the hot pavement.

Very few chips get stolen now!

Dutch helps nervous patients feel calm in the dentist's chair. He sits on their laps and takes their minds off what's happening.

A cuddle from Dutch makes a trip
to the dentist a lot more fun!

Bazz is trained to sniff out a disease called American Foulbrood, which kills bees. He can detect the disease early before all the hives become infected, and he wears a custom-made beekeeper suit so he won't get stung on the job.

Bazz has saved the lives of thousands of bees with his super-sniffer snout.

WATER RESCUE DOG

Name: Reef

Breed: Newfoundland

Location: Italy

Reef patrols the beach with her lifeguard trainer, watching for anyone in danger in the water. If she spots someone who needs rescuing, she races in and helps them swim back to shore. She also jumps out of helicopters and off boats to save people in trouble at sea.

Reef and her team save around twenty lives every year!

The schoolkids

Haze sits with schoolchildren while they read, and plays with them at lunchtime. His calm nature helps students, staff and parents cope with grief and anxiety.

love giving Haze lots of pats and cuddles.

Eba is a scientist! Her main job is to sniff out whale poo in the water. When she finds it, she uses body signals to alert her handler. Human scientists then collect samples, which they use to monitor the health, movement and diet of orca whales.

When it comes to saving whales,
Eba's nose leads the way!

BAT DOG
Name: Finn
Breed: Black Labrador
Location: USA
LAS VEG

Finn is a team player. When a player throws the bat down after hitting the ball, it's Finn's job to retrieve it. He has to be extra focused so he doesn't pick up the baseball instead of the bat! On hot days, he even takes bottles of water to the umpires.

The crowd sometimes cheer louder for Finn than they do for the players!

Yuki works as a search and rescue dog at a ski resort.

Yuki is very intelligent and uses his excellent sense of smell to search for people lost in the snowfields or missing in an avalanche. Once he finds someone, Yuki barks to alert his handler and then starts digging until he reaches them.

Ralf, the therapy dog, visits children staying in hospital. A visit from this gentle giant is a happy, waggy-tailed comfort for patients who are missing home.

Ralf brings smiles to their faces
and calmness to the ward.

PENGUIN PROTECTOR
Name: Mezzo
Breed: Maremma Sheepdog
Location: Australia

Mezzo patrols Middle Island in Victoria with his team, keeping an eye on the penguins that live and breed there. Dogs like Mezzo have a strong instinct to protect, which means no foxes, wild dogs or cats are getting close to the penguins on his watch!

Mezzo is a loyal penguin protector.

Riley is a guide dog for an Austrian Paralympian cross-country skier. At the 2022 Beijing Paralympics they won a gold medal in the 1.5-kilometre sprint and a bronze medal in the 10-kilometre free event!

Riley guides his owner
through the snowy terrain
when competing and training.

Bear is trained to track koalas in the wild.

Bear's unique skill is especially useful after a devastating bush fire. Finding injured koalas who need help can be tricky for humans, but Bear can smell what humans can't see. He has detected over one hundred at-risk koalas!

Ken is employee of the month –

Ken-kun sells delicious sweet potatoes from his stand. He is an excellent shop manager and attracts people with his happy smile. Ken can't take the coins with his paws (or do maths), so customers choose a potato and then place the correct change in a slot. Ken and his owner donate some of the money to animal rescue groups.

every month!

Bravo, Messi!

Messi is a movie star! He trains hard for every role. He has walked the red carpets at the Oscars and the Cannes Film Festival, rubbed noses with some of the biggest actors in the world, and even won the Palm Dog award for his first ever film.

Teddy keeps his owner company while she paints up the illustrations that turn into picture books. He brings her toys and gives lots of hugs, but he has also been known to steal expensive tubes of paint off her desk!

What job could your dog do?

Huge thanks to Erica Wagner, Susannah Chambers and Sucheta Raj at Allen & Unwin for making this book happen and for all your wonderful help and expertise along the way. – MH

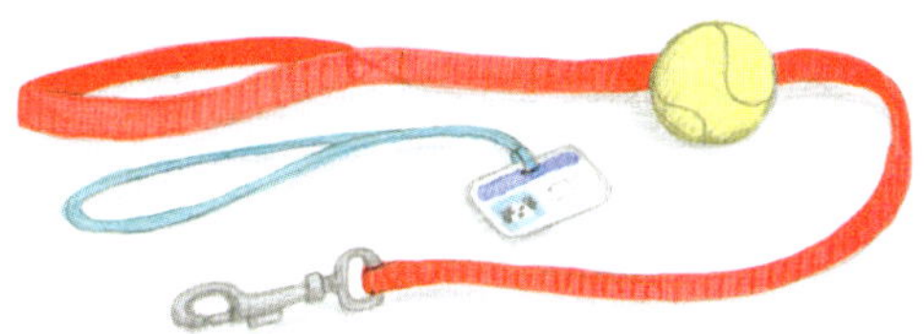

First published by Albert Street Books, an imprint of Allen & Unwin, in 2025

Allen & Unwin
Cammeraygal Country
83 Alexander Street
Crows Nest NSW 2065
Australia
Phone: (61 2) 8425 0100
Email: info@allenandunwin.com
Web: www.allenandunwin.com

Allen & Unwin acknowledges the Traditional Owners of the Country on which we live and work. We pay our respects to all Aboriginal and Torres Strait Islander Elders, past and present.

EU Authorised Representative: Easy Access System Europe, Mustamäe tee 50, 10621 Tallinn, Estonia, gpsr.requests@easproject.com

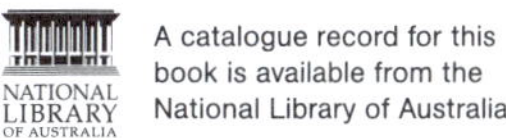

A catalogue record for this book is available from the National Library of Australia

ISBN 978 1 76118 101 6

For teaching resources, explore allenandunwin.com/learn

Cover and text design by Hana Kinoshita Thomson
Set in 12pt Geologica by Hana Kinoshita Thomson
Printed in June 2025 by C&C Offset Printing Co. Ltd, China

1 3 5 7 9 10 8 6 4 2

MML-001